The Earth

Angela Royston

Heinemann Interactive Library
Des Plaines, Illinois

Contents

© 1998 Reed Educational & Professional Publishing
Published by Heinemann Interactive Library, an imprint of Reed Educational & Professional Publishing,
1350 East Touhy Avenue, Suite 240 West
Des Plaines, Illinois 60018

Library of Congress Cataloging-in-Publication Data
Royston, Angela.
    The earth/Angela Royston; illustrated by Jonathan Adams.
        p. cm. — (Inside and out)
    Includes bibliographical references (p. —) and index.
    Summary: Introduces the geology, climate, and different environments of the earth.
    ISBN 1-57572-179-1 (lib. bdg.)
    1. Earth sciences — Juvenile literature. [1. REarth. 2. Earth sciences.]
I. Adams, Jon (Jonathan), ill. II. Title. III. Series.
QE29.R79 1997   97-19334
550 — dc21   CIP
                                                       AC

Photo credits: page 6: ZEFA-Pacific Stock © Reggie David; page 7: Tony Stone Worldwide © Chris Harvey; page 8: Bruce Coleman
Limited © 1993 John Cancalosi; pages 9 and 17: ZEFA; page 10: Britstock-IFA © Eric Bach; page 16: Tony Stone Images ©
Lori Adamski Peek, page 18: © David Hiser, and page 21: © Sally Mayman; page 23: Bruce Coleman © M P L Fogden.

Some words are shown in bold, **like this**. You can find out what they mean
by looking in the glossary. The glossary also helps you say difficult words.

Printed and bound in Italy.
See-through pages printed by SMIC, France.

02 01 00 99 98
10 9 8 7 6 5 4 3 2 1

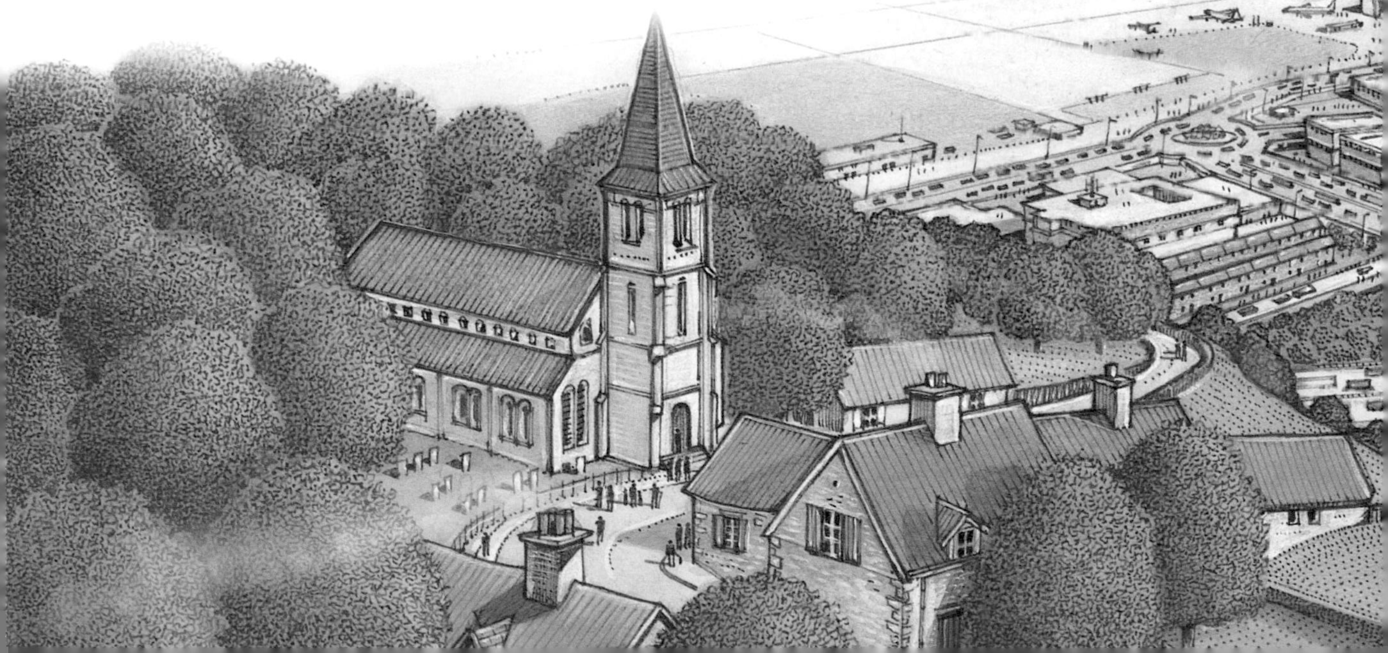

Our Earth

The earth is a huge, round ball that spins through space. This is what the earth looks like from a spacecraft. Can you see the land, the oceans, and the clouds?

A map shows you what the earth would look like if you could make it flat. There are seven **continents**. Where do you live?

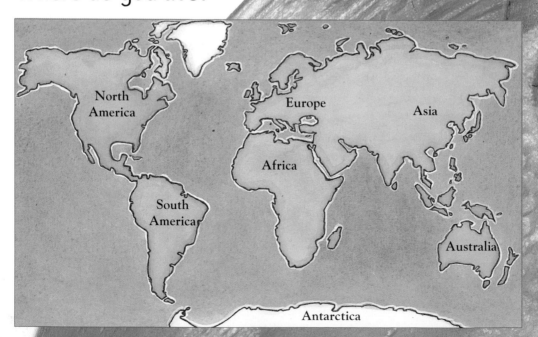

North America

Europe

Asia

Africa

South America

Australia

Antarctica

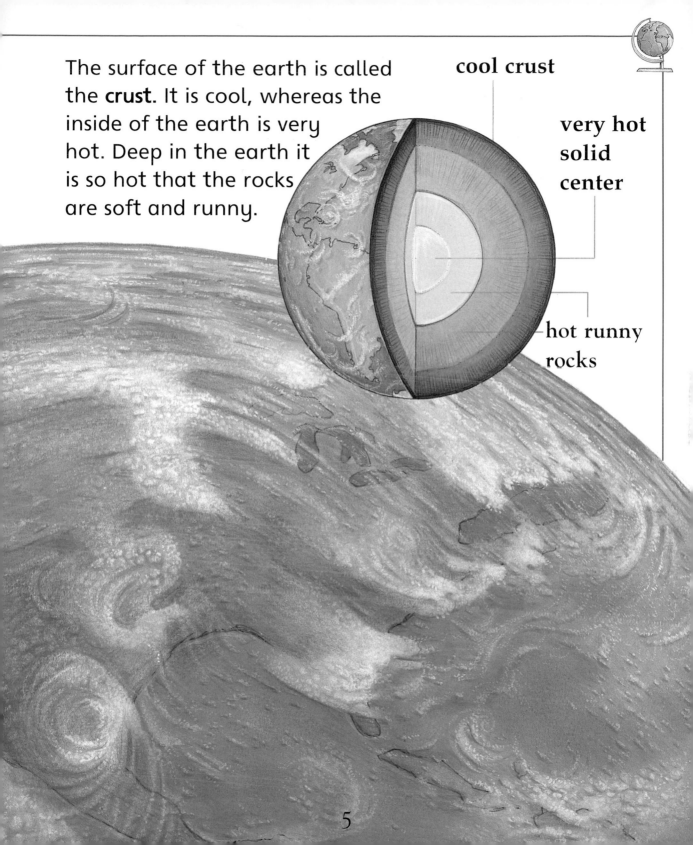

The surface of the earth is called the **crust**. It is cool, whereas the inside of the earth is very hot. Deep in the earth it is so hot that the rocks are soft and runny.

cool crust

very hot solid center

hot runny rocks

High and Low

Some of the land on the earth is low and flat, but in other places it forms high mountains and deep valleys. Most mountain tops are snowy. Some people like to climb them. Others go up on a chairlift and then ski down.

This **volcano** in Hawaii is erupting! Red-hot rock from inside the earth, called **lava,** flows down the mountain. Many mountains were once volcanoes.

Flat grasslands stretch for hundreds of miles across the plains of Africa. Many birds and wild animals, such as these gentle antelope, live there.

Under the Ground

There are amazing things beneath the ground. People drill deep into the earth's **crust** to look for precious stones, metals, coal, and oil.

Coal and oil are found in some layers of rock. Miners travel deep underground to dig coal.

This huge **ruby** was dug from the ground. It will be cut into smaller stones and polished.

Power stations burn oil and coal to make **electricity**. Without electricity, there would be no lights or television!

Spelunkers are people who like to explore caves. Where are these people going?

Many animals dig homes in the ground. This rabbit cares for her babies in the burrow.

 The Land

People have used the land on earth in many ways. At one time it was covered with fields and forests. Farmers grew **crops** and kept animals in the fields. Now, many trees have been cut down and cities have been built.

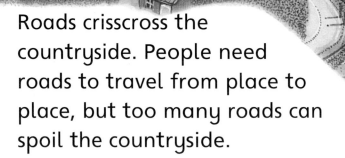

Roads crisscross the countryside. People need roads to travel from place to place, but too many roads can spoil the countryside.

Drop your empty bottles in the **recycling bin**. They will be crushed and made into new ones. Glass, metal cans, and paper can all be recycled.

Earthquake!

Sometimes the solid ground beneath our feet shakes and trembles. Usually, we hardly notice, but in some parts of the world, the shaking can be very violent. The ground cracks and buildings sway.

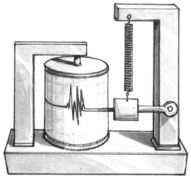

Scientists use special instruments, like this, to measure how strong an earthquake is.

Sometimes an earthquake under the sea makes a huge wave called a tsunami. The wave hits the shore and smashes boats and floods towns all along the coast.

Only a few buildings are left standing. They were built in a way to make them safe. What has happened to the road?

Rainwater

When it rains in the cold, high mountains, the rain freezes into ice. As the ice melts, the water runs down the mountains and into small streams. These streams join to make a river.

Rain puddles soon dry up as the water goes back into the air to form clouds. The wind blows the clouds and the rain falls again somewhere else.

Rain fills lakes and **reservoirs**. Some of the water is carried in pipes to our homes. People can also sail on the reservoir.

When the weather is very cold, it snows instead of rains. Snowflakes are frozen drops of water.

The Weather

The earth is surrounded by air. You cannot see the air, but you can feel it when the wind blows. It is fun to have a picnic on a warm, sunny day, but can you see the dark clouds coming?

When the clouds cannot carry any more water, the water falls as rain. Then people run for shelter. Who will get the wettest?

Thunderstorms can be very frightening. The lightning flashes through the sky towards the ground. A rumble of **thunder** follows each flash of lightning.

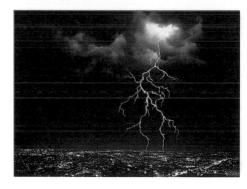

Oceans

More than half of the earth is covered by water. Fish and other animals live in the oceans. This boat is catching fish for people to eat.

There are even mountains under the sea! Some of them are so high the tops appear above the water to form **islands**.

Can you see the holes in these cliffs? They are made by the sea wearing away the rocks. Waves crash against the coast and change the shape of the land.

Deserts

It hardly ever rains in the desert. Very few plants grow there because they need water to survive. Many animals in the desert live under the ground because it is so hot.

Desert winds blow sand into **dunes**. They look like huge waves. Some deserts are rocky and stony, instead of sandy.

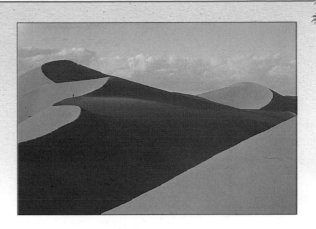

Travelers head toward the **oasis**. This is one of the few places in the desert where there is water. Camels will get a drink there.

Rainforests

Some parts of the world get a lot of rain. Plants grow easily there. They grow so thick and tall, they form huge rainforests. Many animals live there, too. Can you spot the snake and the crocodile?

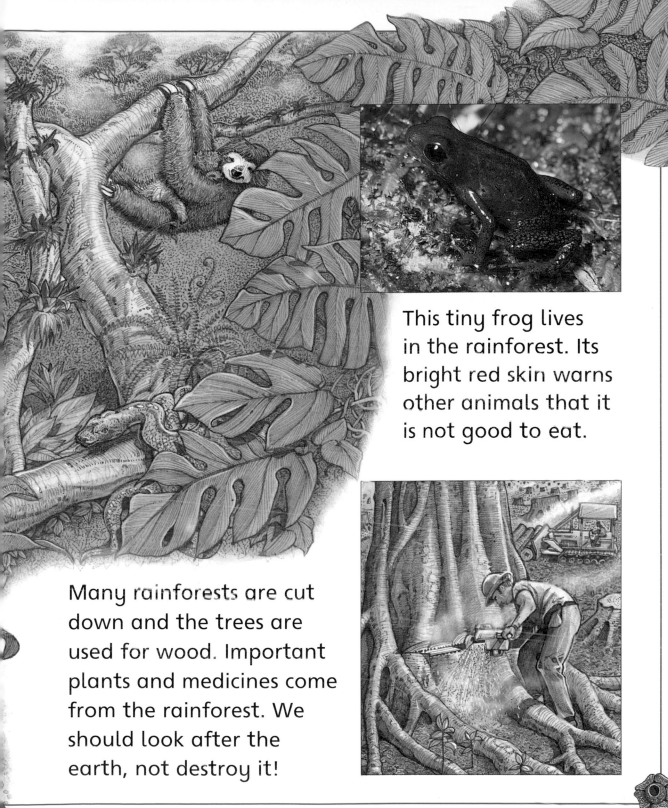

This tiny frog lives in the rainforest. Its bright red skin warns other animals that it is not good to eat.

Many rainforests are cut down and the trees are used for wood. Important plants and medicines come from the rainforest. We should look after the earth, not destroy it!

Glossary

continents	These are huge areas of land.
crops	These are plants grown for food.
crust	This is a hard outer surface.
dunes	These are hills of sand.
electricity	This is energy that can be changed into heat and light.
islands	These are pieces of land surrounded by sea.
lava	This is hot, runny rock from below the Earth's crust. It erupts from volcanoes.
oasis	This is a place in the desert that has water and plants.
recycling	This means reusing glass, paper, or metal to make new things.
reservoirs	These are large lakes for storing water.
ruby	This is a precious red stone.
thunder	This is a loud noise heard after a lightning flash.
volcano	This is a hole in the earth's crust where lava bursts out.

More Books To Read

Dixon, Debra. *The Earth.*
   New York: Dorling Kindersley, 1994.
Wood, Tim. *Our Planet Earth.* New York:
   Simon & Schuster Childrens, 1992.

Index